Landauer Books

Quilting our Just Desserts

by Retta Warehime

Copyright© 2004 by Landauer Corporation

Projects Copyright© 2004 by Retta Warehime

This book was designed, produced, and published by Landauer Books
A division of Landauer Corporation
12251 Maffitt Road, Cumming, Iowa 50061

President/Publisher: Jeramy Lanigan Landauer
Director of Operations: Kitty Jacobson
Editor-in-Chief: Becky Johnston
Creative Director: Laurel Albright
Photographers: Craig Anderson and Dennis Kennedy
Photostylists: Margaret Sindelar & Debbie Burgraff

ISBN: 1-890621-72-2
This book is printed on acid-free paper.
Printed in USA

10 9 8 7 6 5 4 3 2 1

introduction

Get ready to be inspired by country-flavor quilts and
bonus gift ideas to make for special occasions
throughout the year—
from Valentine's Day to Christmas. Celebrate the seasons
with seven wonderful quilts inspired by favorite family
pies along with ideas for easy handcrafted
recipe cards and coordinated quilt labels for gift-giving.

Just for fun you'll find kitchen-and-taste tested recipes
for the fruit pies and nine quick-to-make quilted
projects for home accessories such as table
runners, placemats, potholders, and even a patchwork pillow.

As I designed each fruit-inspired collection,
I had a special friend in mind to be the recipient of the quilt,
accessories, recipe card, and quilt label.
On the following pages, treat yourself (and friends and family)
to seven fantastic quilts each accompanied by
a fruit pie taste sensation and get ready for the
compliments and gratitude that will come your way.

I hope you enjoy quilting our just desserts as much as I did.
Have fun quilting, crafting, and taste-testing the recipes!

Retta Warehime

contents

40 Blueberry Bounty

50 Apple Harvest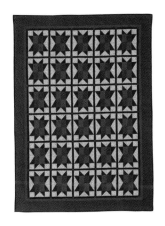

60 Pumpkin Patch

72 Strawberry Surprise

acknowledgments

I wish to thank the great team of cooks and quilters who helped take this book from a dream to reality:

With the exception of one: All quilts quilted by Pam Clarkc
                                            All quilts constructed by Retta Warehime

Cherry Delight was made and quilted by my daughter Shawna Holland and given to me.

Key Lime Twist is being given to Becky Hagensicker – Kennewick, WA.

Lemon sunburst Pie is being given to Pam Clarke – Spokane, WA.

Blueberry Bounty is being given to Kegan Ballard – Burbank, WA.

Apple Harvest is being given to Patty Wagner – Kennewick, WA.

Pumpkin Patch is being given to Barb Ward – Pasco, WA.

Strawberry Surprise is being donated to the American Cancer Center, as a fund raiser, in the name of Terry Tannenburg - Kennewick WA.

The pies were made by a great team of cooks using family recipes. Many thanks to Laila Messerly and Myra Brubaker for their culinary contribution,

general instructions

Before You Begin
Included is information for successfully completing your quilts. To get the most from this book, I suggest that you read once through the following text. Read through the instructions thoroughly before beginning the projects. There are a variety of large and small projects for the beginner as well as the advanced quilter.

Fabrics
I always use 100 percent cotton fabrics. A good rule of thumb in selecting fabric for a quilting project is to buy the best you can afford (although the *most* expensive fabric is not necessarily the best).

Yardage requirements for all the projects in this book are based on 42"-wide fabrics.

Pre-wash all fabrics to test for colorfastness and dry completely to shrink.

Supplies
To machine piece, you'll need a sewing machine that is in good working condition, a walking foot or darning foot for machine quilting, and a quarter inch foot to ensure accurate 1/4" seam allowances.

You will need a rotary cutter, cutting mat, and clear acrylic ruler. Rotary-cutting rulers are available in a variety of sizes, my favorite is the 6" x 12".

Use a good quality, all-purpose cotton thread. The stitching is always more even if the bobbin is wound from the same thread that is used on top. I use cream, white, and gray thread most often.

Use a new needle for each new project. For machine piecing, a size 10/70 or 12/80 works best. For machine quilting, use a 12/80 or 14/90.

My favorite pins are long with yellow heads. Try different sizes, your preference may be different.

Use sharp scissors for cutting fabric, craft scissors to cut paper, fusible web, and template plastic, and small sharp scissors for cutting threads.

The seam ripper, my best friend, is always at my side. I use one every time I sew. Cut every fourth or fifth stitch, then pull the one long thread from the other side. The sharper the seam ripper the better.

A variety of tools are available to mark fabric when tracing around templates or marking quilting designs. Always test your marker on a scrap of fabric to make sure you can remove the marks easily.

Rotary Cutting
All measurements include standard 1/4"-wide seam allowances. If you are unfamiliar with rotary cutting be sure and go to your local quilt shop and ask for help. Use a size and design that fits your hand and that has a lock to cover the blade when it is not in use. Keep an extra blade on hand to ensure that you always have a sharp blade for accurate cutting.

Accuracy is important when machine piecing and matching points is not always easy. When ever possible, work with opposing seam allowances. This way the seams "lock" into position and line up exactly. Sometimes I find it necessary to change my pressing direction as the block is assembled to achieve opposing seams. Pin seam allowances in place if necessary.

Pressing
The traditional rule in quilt making is to press seams to one side, toward the darker color wherever possible. First press the seams flat from the wrong side of the fabric (I call this a tack press); then press the seams in the desired direction from the right side. Press carefully to avoid distorting the shapes. Remember, there are always exceptions to the rule and it may be necessary to repress as you assemble your block or rows.

Templates
When making a template, place the template plastic over the pattern piece and trace with a fine-line permanent marker. Do not add seam allowances. Cut out the templates to the inside the drawn line. You need only one template for each shape. You can make a reverse template or simply flip the same template over to get the reverse. Write the pattern name and grain-line arrow on the template.

Squaring Up Blocks
After stitching your quilt blocks together, take the time to square them up. Make sure the size is 1/2" larger than the finished size. If your blocks vary slightly in size, trim the larger blocks to match the size of the smallest block. Be sure to trim all four sides; otherwise, your block will be lopsided. If your blocks are not the correct finished size, other components of the quilt will need to be adjusted.

general instructions

Straight-Set Quilts

Arrange the blocks as shown in the illustrations provided with each quilt, then sew blocks together in horizontal or vertical rows, according to the quilt instructions. Press the seams in opposite directions from row to row (unless otherwise directed).

Diagonally Set Quilts

Arrange the blocks, setting triangles, and corner triangles as shown in the illustration provided with each quilt. The setting triangles and corner triangles will be larger than necessary and will be trimmed 1/4" from points when the quilt top is completed. Sew the blocks and setting triangles together in diagonal rows; press the seams in opposite directions from row to row (unless directed otherwise). Sew the rows together, matching seams. Sew corner triangles last.

To trim 1/4" from the points it is easiest to use a 24" acrylic ruler and rotary cutter. Simply place the 1/4" line of the ruler on the points of the block (this leaves a 1/4" seam allowance on the edge of the quilt). The instructions will indicate from which block to measure. Cut from block to block all around the outside of the quilt. After trimming, to prevent stretching sew 1/8" basting stitch around the outside.

Borders

For best results, always measure your quilt through the center before cutting or adding border strips. Quilts tend to grow on the outside edges as they are pieced, but remain the same through the center. All of the quilts in this book call for plain border strips. The strips are cut along the crosswise grain and seamed where extra length is needed. Measurements are given for cutting the borders in all of the instructions, these measurements have been mathematically figured, but I find it best to measure through the center.

Measure the length of the quilt top through the center. From the crosswise grain, cut 2 border strips to that measurement, piecing as necessary. Mark the centers of the quilt edges and border strips. Pin the side borders to opposite sides of the quilt top, matching centers and ends and easing as necessary. Sew the border strips to the quilt top; press the seam allowances toward the borders.

Measure the width of the quilt top through the center, including the side borders just added. From the crosswise grain, cut 2 border strips to that measurement, piecing as necessary. Mark the centers of the quilt edges and the border strips. Pin the borders to the top and bottom edges of the quilt top, matching the center marks and ends and easing as necessary. Sew the border strips in place. Press the seams toward the border strips.

Layering and Basting the Quilt

After you complete the quilt top and mark it for quilting, layer the quilt backing, wrong side up, batting, then quilt top. The quilt backing and batting should be cut at least 4" to 6" larger than the quilt top. For large quilts, it is usually necessary to sew 2 or 3 lengths of fabric together to make a backing that is large enough. I sew the backing together with the seam going width-wise instead of lengthwise to get optimum use of the fabric. Always trim away the selvages before piecing the lengths together. Press the seams open to make quilting easier by minimizing bulk.

Spread the backing wrong side up on a flat, clean surface. Anchor it with pins or masking tape. Be careful not to stretch the backing out of shape. Spread the batting over the backing, smoothing wrinkles from the center out. Center the pressed quilt top on top of the batting. Again, smoothing wrinkles from the center out, making sure the quilt-top edges are parallel to the edges of the backing. Beginning in the center, baste with needle and thread and work diagonally to each corner. Then baste a grid of horizontal and vertical lines 6" to 8" apart. You can also baste the layers with #2 rustproof safety pins. Place pins about 6" to 8" apart and remove safety pins as you go.

For any machine quilting it is extremely helpful to have a walking foot to help feed the quilt layers through the machine without shifting or puckering. Some machines have a built-in walking foot; most machines require a separate attachment.

For free-motion quilting, you need a darning foot and the ability to drop or cover the feed dogs on your machine. Consult your sewing machine instruction manual if you need help. With free-motion quilting, you guide the fabric in the direction of the design rather than turning the fabric under the needle. This does take some practice.

Binding

I prefer French double-fold binding. All bindings in this book were cut 2-1/2" wide across the width of fabric and then pieced.

Trim the batting and backing even with the quilt top. RST, at right angles, stitch corner to corner. Trim leftover fabric 1/4" from seam and press all seams open.

Fold the binding strip in half lengthwise, wrong sides together, and press. Measure the quilt top vertically through the center and cut 2 strips of binding to this length for side bindings. Use a 1/4" seam allowance to stitch the binding to the side edges of the quilt, keeping the raw edges of binding even with the trimmed edges of quilt.

Fold the binding over the edges of the quilt to the back of the quilt, with the folded edge covering the row of machine stitching. Hand stitch the binding in place. Measure the quilt top horizontally through the center and cut 2 strips from binding to this measurement, plus 1". Fold under and press 1/2" on each end of binding. Stitch the binding to the top and bottom of the quilt, keeping raw edges even with quilt top edges. Fold the binding to the backside and finish the same as the side bindings. Slipstitch the ends closed.

Finishing Up

All of the quilts in this book were quilted by a long-arm machine quilter. To find a long-arm quilter in your area, check with your local quilt shop for referrals.

Signing Your Quilt

Please be sure to sign and date your quilts. It is important to include the name of the quilt, your name the quilter's name and your city and state, the date, and the intended recipient. By documenting your quilt with something as simple as a label, future generations will be able to learn a little bit of its history.

Use a fine-tipped, permanent fabric marker to record all of the information on a piece of fabric; attach it to the back of the quilt with small stitches or blanket stitch it in place. You may also type or embroider your information on fabric before attaching to the back of your finished quilt.

Cherry Delight

Fall in love with cherries in a quilt, pie, and tart-in-a-heart gift collection.

Cherry Delight Quilt

Cherry Delight Quilt

Finished Size: 32-1/2" x 32-1/2"
Finished Block: 8" x 8"

Supplies

2 yards Background

1/3 yard Red #1

1-1/2 yards Red #2

1/4 yard Red #3

3/4 yard Red #4

1-1/4 yard Backing

Cutting

Background
- 2—1-1/2" x 42" strips cut into 40—1-1/2" squares (on 20 - 1-1/2" squares, on wrong side of the fabric draw a line once on the diagonal)
- 10—1-7/8" squares (on wrong side of the fabric, draw a line once on the diagonal)
- 3—2-1/2" x 42" strips cut into 40—2-1/2" x 1-1/2" pieces
- 5—4-1/2" squares
- 1—8" square cut once on the diagonal for corner triangles
- 1—14" square cut twice on the diagonal for setting triangles

Red #1
- 5—1-1/2" x 42" strips cut into 20—1-1/2" squares (on wrong side of the fabric draw a line once on the diagonal) and 50—2-1/2" x 1-1/2" pieces

Red #2
- 3—1-1/2" x 42" strips cut into 60—1-1/2" squares (on wrong side of the fabric draw a line once on the diagonal)
- 10—1-7/8" squares
- 16—1" x 8 1/2" strips (sashing)
- 2—1" x 26" sides (accent)
- 2—1" x 26" top and bottom (accent)
- 4—2-1/2" x 42" strips (binding)

Red #3
- 2—1-1/2" x 42" strips cut into 20—1-1/2" squares (on wrong side of the fabric draw a line once on the diagonal) and 10—2-1/2" x 1-1/2" pieces

Red #4
- 2—2-1/2" x 42" strips cut into 20—2-1/2" x 1-1/2" pieces
- 16—1" squares (corner stones)
- 2—3-1/2" x 27" sides
- 2—3-1/2" x 33" top and bottom

Sewing

1. RST, pair up 1-7/8" Red #2 and 1-7/8" background squares. Sew 1/4" each side of the drawn line. Cut apart on the drawn line and press towards red. Make 20—Units 1.

Make 20
Unit 1

2. RST, on the drawn line, sew 1-1/2" Red #1 squares to left side of 2-1/2" x 1-1/2" background pieces. Cut away 1/4" from sewn line and press towards red. Repeat for right side using 1-1/2" Red #2 squares. Press towards red. Make 10—Units 2.

#1
2-1/2"
  #2

2-1/2" x 1-1/2"

Make 10
Unit 2

3. RST, on the drawn line, sew 1-1/2" Red #2 squares to left side of 2-1/2" x 1-1/2" background pieces. Cut away 1/4" from sewn line and press towards red. Repeat for right side using 1-1/2" Red #3 squares. Press towards red. Make 10—Units 3.

#2
1-1/2"
  #3

2-1/2" x 1-1/2" Bkg

Make 10
Unit 3

4. RST, on the drawn line, sew 1-1/2" background squares to left side of 2-1/2" x 1-1/2" Red #3 pieces. Cut away 1/4" from sewn line and press to background. Repeat for right side using 1-1/2" Red #1 squares. Press to red #3. Make 10—Units 4.

1-1/2"
  #1

#3   2-1/2" x 1-1/2"

Make 10
Unit 4

5. RST, on the drawn line, sew 1-1/2" Red #3 squares to left side of 2-1/2" x 1-1/2" Red #1 pieces. Cut away 1/4" from sewn line and press to Red #1. Repeat for right side using 1-1/2" background squares. Press to background. Make 10—Units 5.

#3
1-1/2"
  #2

#1   2-1/2" x 1-1/2"

Make 10
Unit 5

6. RST, on the drawn line, sew 2-1/2" x 1-1/2" Red #4 to right side of 2-1/2" x 1-1/2" Red #1 pieces. Cut away 1/4" from sewn line and press to Red #1. Sew 2-1/2" x 1-1/2" Red #1 to right side of Red #4. Press to Red #1. Add 1-1/2" Red #2 squares to each end of unit. Press to Red # 2. Make 20—Units 6.

#1
2-1/2" x 1-1/2"
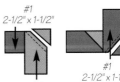 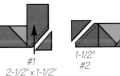

#4
2-1/2" x 1-1/2"

#1
2-1/2" x 1-1/2"

1-1/2"   1-1/2"
#2   #2

Make 20
Unit 6

Assemble the Block

1. Row 1 and 5 are the same. Using 1-1/2" background squares, 2-1/2" x 1-1/2" background piece and units 2 and 3, assemble 10 rows. Press seams toward background.

1-1/2"   Unit 2   2-1/2" x 1-1/2"   Unit 3   1-1/2"

Assemble 10 rows: 5—Row 1; 5—Row 5

2. Row 2 and 4 are the same. Using units 4, 5, and 6, assemble 10 rows. Press seams toward Units 4 and 5.

Unit 4   Unit 6   Unit 5

Assemble 10 rows: 5—Row 2; 5—Row 4

3. Make row 3 using Units 1 and 2-1/2" x 1-1/2" background pieces. Press to background. Make 10 rows.

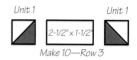

Unit 1   Unit 1

2-1/2" x 1-1/2"

Make 10—Row 3

4. Assemble rows in the following order:
   Sew rows 1 to rows 2. Press towards row 1
   Sew rows 4 to rows 5. Press towards row 5
   Sew rows 3 to Units 6. Press towards row 3. Sew these two units to opposite sides of 4-1/2"center squares. Press towards center square.

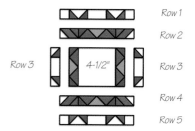

Row 1
Row 2
Row 3   4-1/2"   Row 3
Row 4
Row 5

5. Sew top and bottom rows to center section to complete the block. Press away from center. Make 5 blocks.

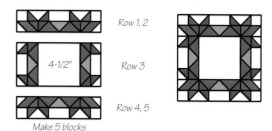

Row 1, 2
4-1/2"   Row 3
Row 4, 5
Make 5 blocks

Assemble the Quilt

1. Sew 1" x 8-1/2" sashing strips to blocks using illustration below. Press towards sashing strips.

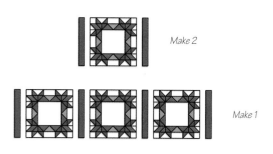

Make 2

Make 1

2. Make two each sashing rows using 1" x 8-1/2" sashing strips and 1" cornerstones. Press towards sashing strips.

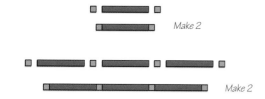

Make 2

Make 2

3. Sew one sashing row to the top of two blocks. Press toward sashing strip. Sew one long sashing row to the top and bottom of the three-block row. Press toward sashing strip.

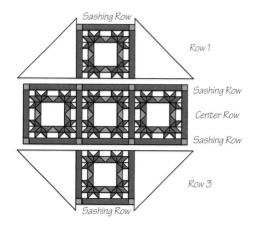

Sashing Row
Row 1
Sashing Row
Center Row
Sashing Row
Row 3
Sashing Row

4. Make row 1 and 3 using setting triangle and single blocks. Make center row using the 3-block row and setting triangles.

5. Join rows and add corner triangles. Trim 1/4" from points. Sew 1/8" all around to prevent stretching.

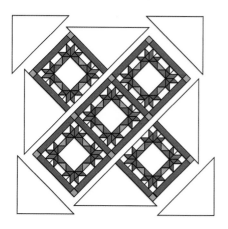

6. Sew 1" cornerstones to each end of both 1" x 26" top and bottom accent border strips.

7. Add 1" accent borders then 3-1/2" outside borders, sides first then top and bottom.

Finishing the Quilt

See General Instructions on page 7 to layer, quilt, and bind.

Cherry Delight Quilt

Cherry Delight Pie

4 cups pitted fresh or canned drained cherries

1-1/2- 2 cups sugar

1/4 cup flour

1/8 tsp. salt

1 pie crust for double-crust pie

2 tbsp. butter

Combine cherries, sugar, flour and salt. Fill 9" pastry-lined pie pan.
Dot with butter and adjust top crust.
Bake in 450° oven 10 minutes, then in 350°oven about 30 minutes. Serves 8.

Recipe Card & Quilt Label

Give your special Valentine a gift to remember when you include a recipe card and attach a quilt label embroidered with your name and the year. You may want to add a border of heart-shaped buttons to the recipe card to make it a Valentine treat from the heart.

Key Lime Twist

Put a new twist
on spring with a little lime
and lots of love!

Key Lime Twist Quilt

Key Lime Twist Quilt

Finished Size: 48" x 69"
Finished Block: 7-1/2"

Supplies

3 yards Background

1 yard each of four different greens

1/2 yard Binding (green)

3 yards Backing

Cutting

Background

- 15—3" squares
- 8—8" squares
- 2—7" squares cut once on the diagonal for corner triangles
- 3—13" squares cut twice on the diagonal for setting triangles
- 4—3-7/8" x 42" strips cut into 32—3-7/8" squares (on the wrong side of the fabric, draw a line once on the diagonal)
- 2—3" x 55-1/2" strips for first side borders
- 2—3" x 39-1/2" strips for first top and bottom borders
- 2—4" x 62-1/2" strips for second side borders
- 2—4" x 48-1/2" strips for second top and bottom borders

Green—from each of the four greens

- 16—3" squares
- 8—3-7/8" squares
- 4—1-1/2" x 42" strips

Binding

- 6—2-1/2" x 42" strips

Sewing

Instructions are for four each one color. Work with one color at a time. You will have one block left to make a pillow or extra project. Total 15 blocks.

1. RST, pair 3-7/8" color squares with 3-7/8" background squares.

3" Half Square Triangles

   A. Sew 1/4" from each side of the diagonal line.

   B. Cut apart on the diagonal line. Each square will make two half square triangles. Square half square triangles to 3".

2. To assemble the blocks, sew half-square triangles, 3" green squares and 3" background squares together in rows. Make eight rows 1 and 3 and four rows 2.

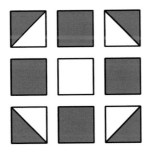

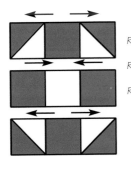

Row 1
Row 2
Row 3

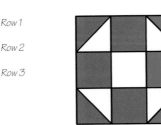

Block Measures 8"

   A. Sew rows together and press to center.

Assembling the Quilt

Lay out blocks for color placement.

1. Using setting triangles and 8" background squares assemble two each rows 1, 2, and 3 and one row 4. Press to background.

   A. Assemble rows, then add corner triangles. Press one direction. See diagonal set quilts in general instructions to trim sides.

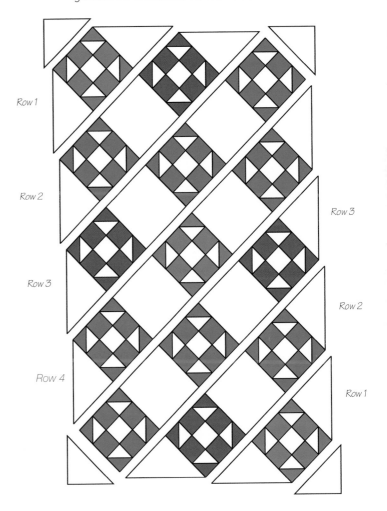

Row 1
Row 2
Row 3
Row 3
Row 4
Row 3
Row 2
Row 1

Making the Pieced Accent Borders

1. Make 4 strip sets using four randomly placed 1-1/2" x 42" green strips in each. Cut into 94—1-1/2" units.

Cut 94—1-1/2" Unit A   Make 4 strip sets

2. Sew 1-1/2" units end to end. Press one direction. Make: 2—34 count strips; 2—41 count strips; 2—53 count strips; 2—60 count strips.

Make 2—34 Count

Make 2—41 Count

Make 2—53 Count

Make 2—60 Count

3. Sew the 53 count strips to each side of the quilt. Press to quilt. Add the 34 count strips to the top and bottom. Press to quilt.

4. Sew the 3" x 55-1/2" borders to each side of the quilt. Press to border. Add the 3" x 39-1/2" borders to the top and bottom. Press to border.

5. Sew the 60 count strips to each side of the quilt. Press to quilt. Add the 41 count strips to the top and bottom. Press to quilt.

6. Sew the 4" x 62-1/2" borders to each side of the quilt. Press to border. Add the 4" x 48-1/2" borders to the top and bottom. Press to border.

4" x 62-1/2"

3" x 55-1/2"

3" x 39-1/2"

4" x 48"

Finishing the Quilt

See General Instructions on page 7 to layer, quilt, and bind.

Key Lime Twist Quilt

Pillow

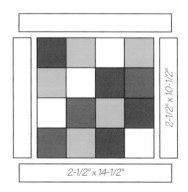

Finished Size: 14" x 14"

Supplies

Scraps or 1/4 yard each light green, medium green, and cream

Dark green—1/4 yard

1—16" square batting

1/2" Cording—1-2/3 yards

Cutting

- Light green: 5—3" squares
- Medium green: 3—3" squares
- Cream: 4—3" squares, 2—2-1/2" x 10-1/2" pieces, and 2—2-1/2" x 14-1/2" pieces
- Dark green: 4—3" squares, 1—2" x 66" bias strip, and 1—14-1/2" square (backing)

Sewing

1. Sew 3" squares together making 4 rows with four squares in each. Press each row in opposite directions and sew together.

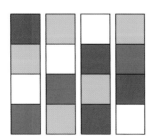
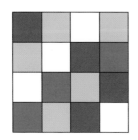

2. Add 2-1/2" x 10-1/2" cream pieces to each side and 2-1/2" x 14-1/2" pieces to the top and bottom. Lay on batting piece and quilt. Trim edges even.

2-1/2" x 10-1/2"

2-1/2" x 14-1/2"

3. With wrong sides together, lay cording in 2" green bias strip and baste together to make piping.

4. Baste piping to pillow front with raw edges even. Trim excess at overlap.

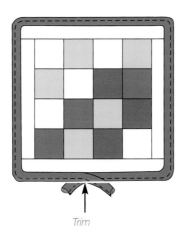

Trim

5. Place pillow top and backing piece, RST. Stitch all around leaving opening for turning.

6. Turn right side out and stuff. Sew opening closed.

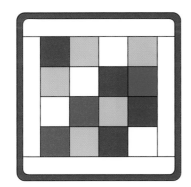

Potholder

Finished Size: 14" x 14"

Supplies

1—Terry Cloth kitchen towel
Coordinating Fabric—1/2 yard
Floss—1 skein

Cutting

- 2—Full size Pattern Pieces A from dishtowel
- 2—3/4 Pattern Pieces A from coordinating fabric,
  1—2-1/2" x 7-1/2" bias strip, and
- 1—2-1/2" x 34" bias strip

Sewing

1. Layer coordinating fabric pieces, wrong sides together. Apply 7-1/2" binding strip to top straight

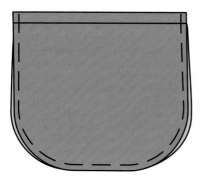

    edge, same as quilt. Baste layers 1/8" from edges around outside edge.

2. Layer kitchen towel pieces, wrong sides together and lay coordinating piece op top, with bottom and side

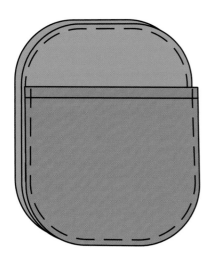

    edges even. Baste all layers 1/8" from edges around outside edge.

3. Bind same as quilt. Cut 12 strands of floss four inches long. Using a large needle, thread floss through top and tie off. Trim end to length desired.

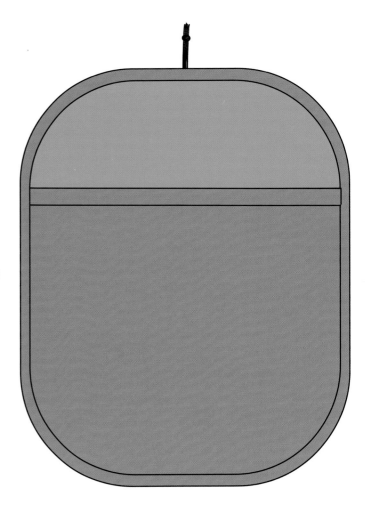

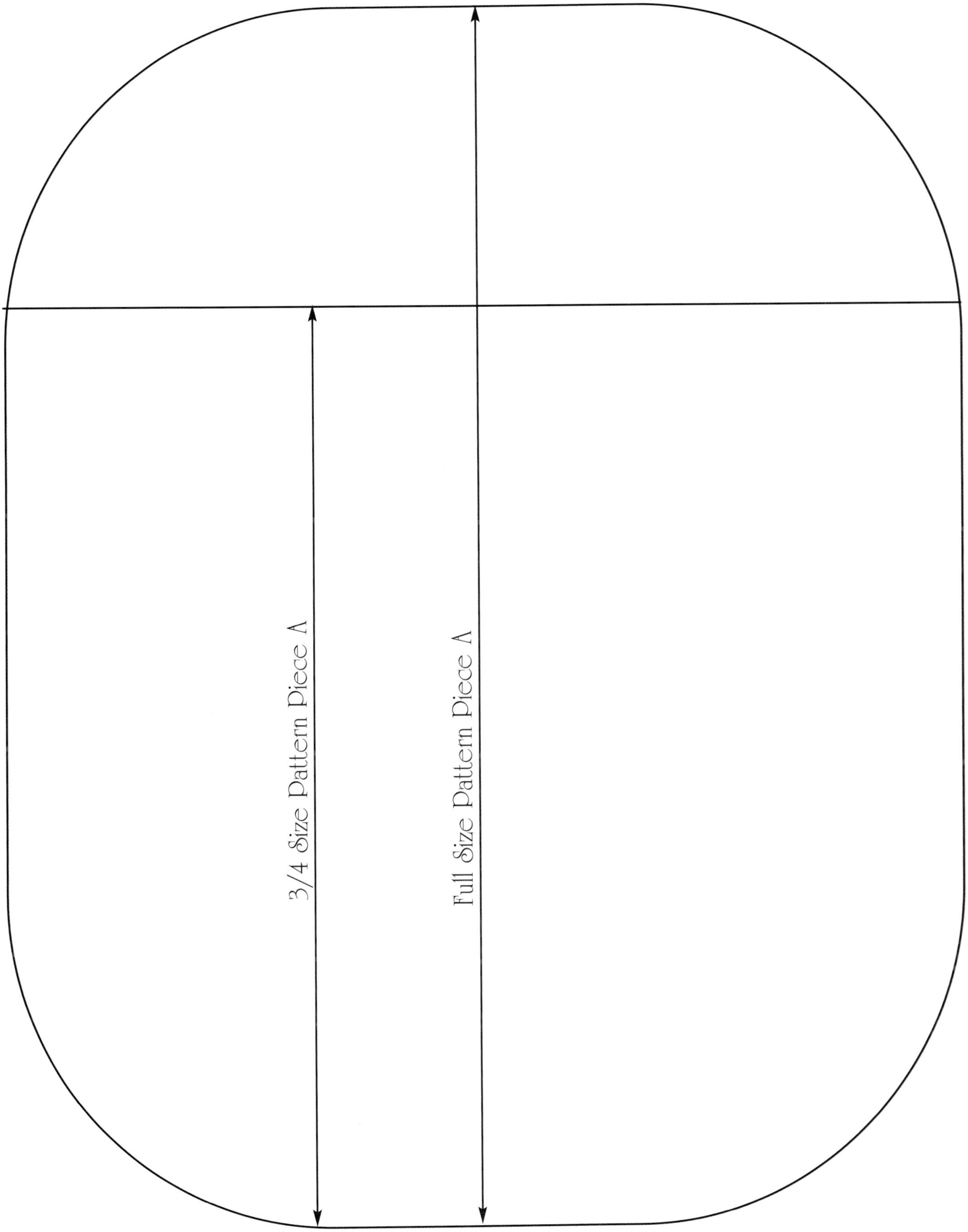

3/4 Size Pattern Piece A

Full Size Pattern Piece A

Key Lime Twist Pie

1 can sweetened condensed milk

1—8oz. container whipped dessert topping

1—6oz. can frozen limeade, thawed

3 drops green food coloring

1 graham cracker crust

In large mixing bowl, combine sweetened condensed milk, whipped desert topping, thawed frozen limeade, and food coloring. Pour into prepared graham cracker crust. Refrigerate 4-6 hours. Serves 8.

Graham Cracker Crust:

Combine 13 crushed graham crackers, 1/3 cup melted butter, and 1/3 cup sugar. Mix well. Press firmly into buttered 9-inch pie pan. Chill until set, about 45 minutes.

Recipe Card & Quilt Label

To make this collection special, tuck a vintage green-glass juice squeezer into the potholder along with the recipe card. You may want to add your favorite meringue recipe as well.

Lemon Sunburst

For a burst of summer sunshine, just add a little lemon to your day.

Lemon Sunburst Quilt

Lemon Sunburst Quilt

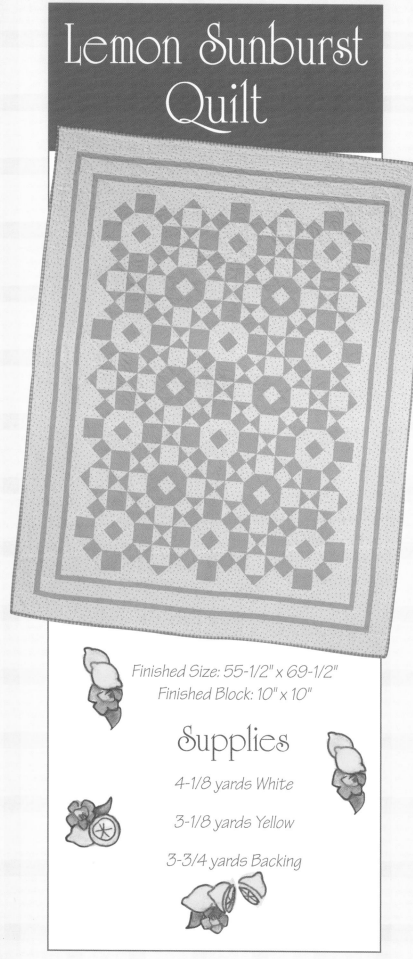

Finished Size: 55-1/2" x 69-1/2"
Finished Block: 10" x 10"

Supplies

4-1/8 yards White

3-1/8 yards Yellow

3-3/4 yards Backing

Cutting

White

- 8—2-1/2" x 42" strips
- 12—2-1/2" x 42" strips cut into 192—2-1/2" squares (on the wrong side of the fabric, draw a line once on the diagonal)
- 4—4-1/2" x 42" strips cut into 34—4-1/2" squares
- 2—8 " squares cut once on the diagonal for corner triangles
- 5—10" squares cut twice on the diagonal for setting triangles
- 2—2-1/2" x 58-1/2" strips for second border - sides
- 2—2-1/2" x 48-1/2" strips for second border - top and bottom
- 2—3-1/2" x 64" strips for fourth border - sides
- 2—3-1/2" x 56" strips for fourth border - top and bottom

Yellow

- 8—2-1/2" strips
- 9—2-1/2" x 42" strips cut into 136—2-1/2" squares (on the wrong side of the fabric draw a line once on the diagonal)
- 6—4-1/2" x 42" strips cut into 48—4-1/2" squares
- 2—1-1/4" x 57" strips for first border - sides
- 2—1-1/4" x 44-1/2" strips for first border - top and bottom
- 2—1-1/4" x 62-1/2" strips for third border - sides
- 2—1-1/4" x 50" strips for third border - top and bottom
- 6—2-1/2" x 42" strips (binding)

Sewing

1. Sew three white and two yellow 2-1/2" x 42" strips together to make one strip set. Cut into 6—2-1/2" Units 1.

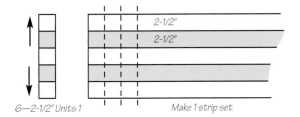

6—2-1/2" Units 1   Make 1 strip set

2. Sew three yellow and two white 2-1/2" x 42" strips together to make one strip set. Cut into 12—2-1/2" Units 2.

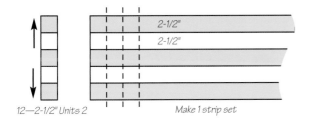

12—2-1/2" Units 2   Make 1 strip set

3. Sew one yellow and one white 2-1/2" x 42" strips together to make three strip sets. Cut into 36—2-1/2" Units 3.

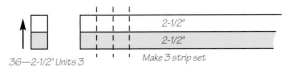

36—2-1/2" Units 3   Make 3 strip set

4. Using 2-1/2" yellow squares, RST, sew on drawn line to opposite corners of 4-1/2" white squares. Trim 1/4" from sewn line. Press out. Repeat for opposite corners. Make 34—Units 4.

34—Units 4

5. Using 2-1/2" white squares, RST, sew on drawn line to opposite corners of 4-1/2" yellow squares. Trim 1/4" from sewn line. Press out. Repeat for opposite corners. Make 48 - Units 5.

48—Units 5

Assemble the Blocks and Setting Triangles

1. Assemble 12 Half Blocks A, using Units 3 and 4.

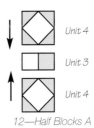

Unit 4

Unit 3

Unit 4

12—Half Blocks A

A. Join Half Blocks with Units 1. Press to Unit 1.

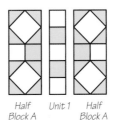 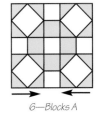

Half Block A   Unit 1   Half Block A   6—Blocks A

2. Assemble 24 Half Blocks B, using Units 3 and 5.

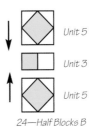

Unit 5

Unit 3

Unit 5

24—Half Blocks B

A. Join Half Blocks with Units 2. Press away from Unit 2.

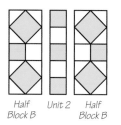 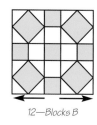

Half Block B   Unit 2   Half Block B   12—Blocks B

Assemble the Quilt

1. Sew rows together using Setting Triangles and alternating Blocks A and Blocks B. Press away from Blocks B and towards Block A. Add corner triangles. Trim 1/4" from Block B points. Stitch 1/8" around outside edges for stability.

3. Sew remaining Units 4, RST, to white Setting Triangles.

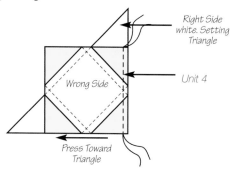

Right Side white. Setting Triangle

Unit 4

Wrong Side

Press Toward Triangle

A. Sew remaining Setting Triangles to other side of Units 4, then trim away excess.

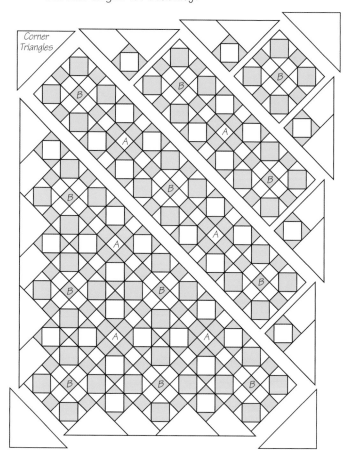

Corner Triangles

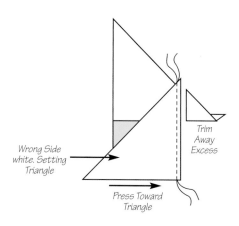

Wrong Side white. Setting Triangle

Trim Away Excess

Press Toward Triangle

2. Add borders, sides first then top and bottom, beginning with first border. Press towards borders one and three.

Finishing the Quilt

See General Instructions on page 7 to layer, quilt, and bind.

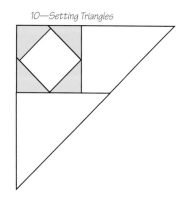

10—Setting Triangles

Lemon Sunburst Quilt

Table Runner

Finished size: 42" x 22"

Supplies

Yellow (w/binding): 3/4 yard

White: 1/3 yard

Yellow Check: 2/3 yard

Backing: 1-1/4 yard

Batting: 44" x 24" piece

Cutting

- Yellow: 5—2-1/2" x 22" strips,
  2—2-1/2" x 10-1/2" pieces (sides),
  2—2-1/2" x 34-1/2" pieces (top and bottom),
  and 4—2-1/2" x 42" strips (binding)

- White: 5—2-1/2" x 22" strips

- Yellow Check: 2—4-1/2" x 14-1/2" (sides),
  and 2—4-1/2" x 42-1/2" (top and bottom)

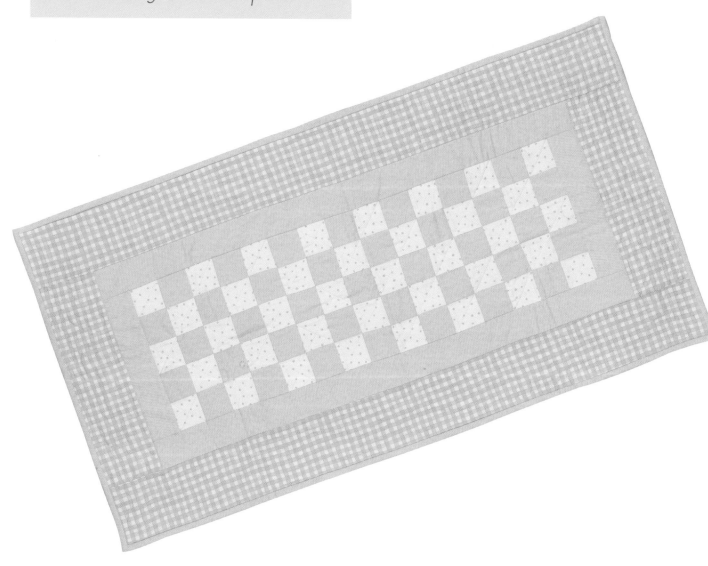

Sewing

1. Make one strip set using 2-1/2" x 22" yellow and white strips. Cut into 8—2-1/2" units A.

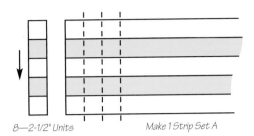

8—2-1/2" Units   Make 1 Strip Set A

2. Make one strip set using 2-1/2" x 22" yellow and white strips. Cut into 7—2-1/2" units B.

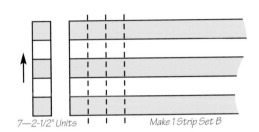

7—2-1/2" Units   Make 1 Strip Set B

3. Sew units together.

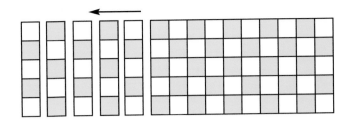

4. Add yellow 2-1/2" side borders then top and bottom. Add yellow check 4-1/2" borders, sides first then top and bottom.

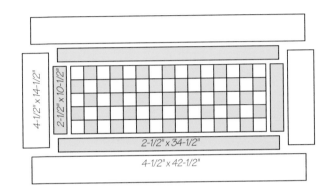

4-1/2" x 14-1/2"

2-1/2" x 10-1/2"

2-1/2" x 34-1/2"

4-1/2" x 42-1/2"

5. Layer, quilt, and bind same as quilt.

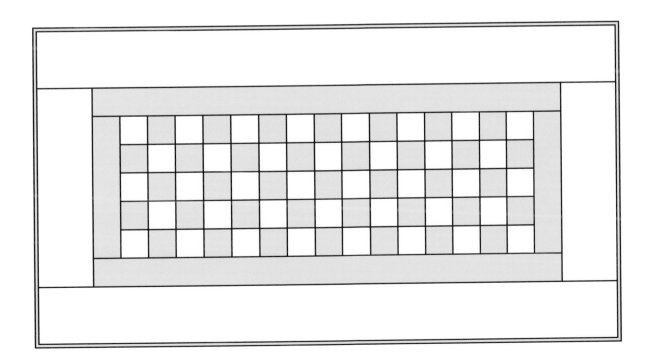

Lemon Sunburst Pie

1 can sweetened condensed milk

1—8oz. container whipped dessert topping

1—6oz. can frozen lemonade, thawed

3 drops yellow food coloring

1 graham cracker crust

In large mixing bowl, combine sweetened condensed milk, whipped dessert topping, thawed frozen lemonade, and food coloring. Pour into prepared graham cracker crust. Refrigerate 4-6 hours. Serves 8.

Graham Cracker Crust:

Combine 13 crushed graham crackers, 1/3 cup melted butter, and 1/3 cup sugar. Mix well. Press firmly into buttered 9-inch pie pan. Chill until set, about 45 minutes.

Recipe Card & Quilt Label

Use the recipe card for a fun picnic or party invitation. Simply add the "you're invited" details to the front of the fold-over card, and then include the recipe inside. Let your guests know that a little bit of sunshine will be ready and waiting when they arrive.

Blueberry Bounty

From pies to pancakes, who can resist the end-of-summer blueberry bounty?

Blueberry Bounty Quilt

Blueberry Bounty Quilt

Finished Size: 69" x 84"
Finished Star Block: 6" x 6"
Finished Chain Block: 9" x 9"

Supplies

5-5/8 yards Background

2-1/4 yards Blue

1/2 yard Blue Center

5 yards Backing

Cutting

Background

- 5—2" x 42" strips cut into 100—2" squares
- 5—3 1/2" strips cut into 100—3-1/2" x 2" pieces
- 6—6-1/2" x 42" strips cut into 20—6-1/2" squares and 10—8" x 6-1/2" pieces
- 4—8" x 42" strips
- 4—6-1/2" x 42" strips
- 4—2" x 42" strips
- 6—3-1/2" x 42" strips
- 3—9-1/2" x 42" strips cut into 30—3-1/2" x 9-1/2" pieces

Blue

- 10—2" x 42" strips cut into 200—2" squares (on wrong side of the fabric, draw a line once on the diagonal)
- 8—2" x 42" strips
- 3—3-1/2" x 42" strips
- 8—2-1/2" strips

Blue Center

- 3—3-1/2" x 42" strips cut into 25—3-1/2" squares

Sewing

Chain Blocks

1. Make the following strip sets, using blue and background strips. Measurements for strips, pressing directions, units to cut and amounts are given with the illustrations.

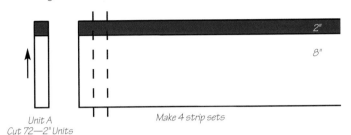

Unit A
Cut 72—2" Units
Make 4 strip sets

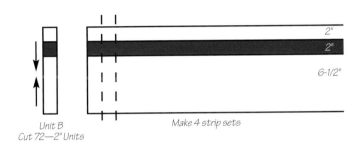

Unit B
Cut 72—2" Units
Make 4 strip sets

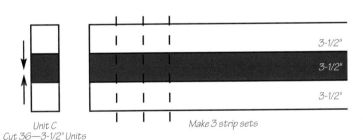

Unit C
Cut 36—3-1/2" Units
Make 3 strip sets

2. Using the illustration below, assemble 36 Chain Blocks.

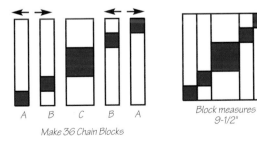

A B C B A

Block measures 9-1/2"

Make 36 Chain Blocks

Star Blocks

1. RST, sew a 2" blue square to the left side of the 3-1/2" x 2" background piece, on the drawn line. Cut away excess 1/4" from drawn line and press to outside. Repeat for right side to make star point units. Make 100 star point units.

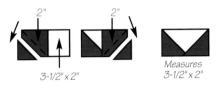

3-1/2" x 2"
Measures 3-1/2" x 2"

2. Sew 2" background square to each side of 50 star point units. Press to background square.

Make 50   Measures —6-1/2"

3. Sew remaining star point units to each side of 3-1/2" blue center squares. Press to inside.

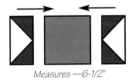

Measures —6-1/2"

4. Sew rows together to make 25 Star Blocks.

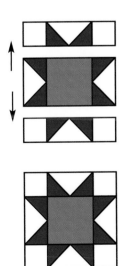

Assembling the Rows

1. Using 8" x 6-1/2" background pieces, 6-1/2" background squares, and star blocks, assemble five star rows. Press to background.

Make 5 rows

2. Using 3-1/2" x 9-1/2" background pieces and alternating Chain Blocks, assemble six chain rows. Press to background.

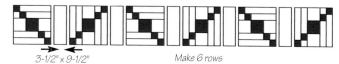

3-1/2" x 9-1/2"   Make 6 rows

3. Alternating rows, assemble the quilt top and press one direction.

Finishing the Quilt

See General Instructions on page 7 to layer, quilt, and bind.

Blueberry Bounty Quilt

Potholder

Finished size: 7 1/2" x 8"

Supplies

Scraps of Light and Dark Blue
1—Terry cloth kitchen towel

Cutting

- Light Blue: 2—8" x 4" pieces and
  1—8" x 5-1/2" piece
- Dark Blue: 1—8" x 2" piece and
  1—2-1/2" x 30" strip bias

Sewing

1. Sew 8" x 4" light blue and 8" x 2" dark
   blue pieces together. Using pattern piece,
   half size C, cut one.

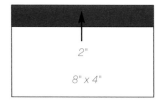
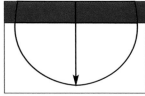

Half size C

A. Using pattern piece half size C and
   8" x 5-1/2" Light blue piece, cut one.

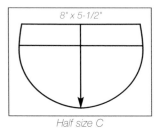

Half size C

B. Place pieces RST, and stitch across top.
   Turn right sides out and press. Stitch pieces
   together under dark blue strip. Baste layers
   1/8" from edges around out side edge.

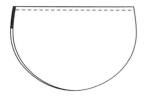

46

2. Using pattern piece, full size C,
   cut two pieces from kitchen towel.

3. Layer top and two towel pieces
   together. Baste all layers 1/8" from
   edges around outside edge.

4. Bind same as quilt, beginning at top
   right corner continuing around, covering
   where you began. Continue and make a
   hanging loop, bringing it to the back side
   of the potholder. Cut binding 1/2" longer,
   fold in the raw edges, and stitch to
   back side.

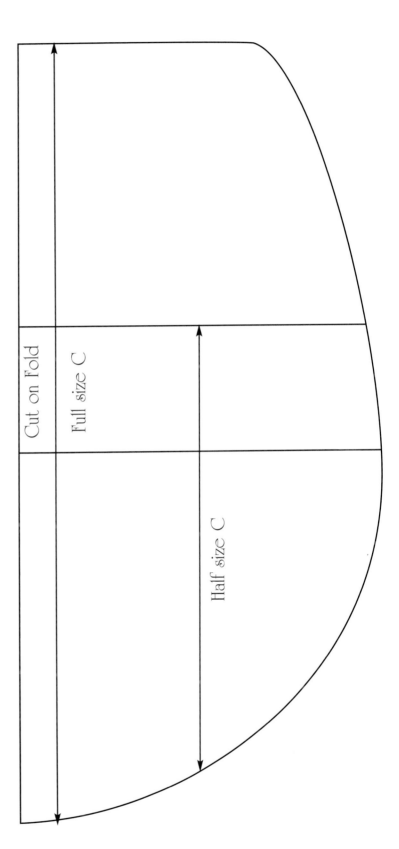

Cut on Fold

Full size C

Half size C

Blueberry Bounty Pie

2-1/2 cups fresh, cannned or frozen blueberries

1 cup sugar

1/4 cup flour

1/8 tsp. salt

1 tbsp. lemon juice

2 tbsp. butter

1 pie crust for double-crust pie

Combine blueberries, sugar, flour, salt and lemon juice. Fill 8" pastry-lined pan. Dot with butter and adjust top crust. Bake in 450° oven 10 minutes, then in 350°oven about 30 minutes. Serves 8.

Pie Crust for Double-Crust Pie

2 1/2 cups flour

3/4 cup shortening

1/2 tsp. salt

5-6 tbsp. ice water

With pastry blender, combine flour, shortening and salt to consistency of coarse meal. Add water, one tablespoon at a time, using fork to work in until a ball can be formed. Form into 2 balls. Turn onto lightly floured surface. Roll to fit pie pan.

Recipe Card & Quilt Label

Visiting friends or family at the cabin on the lake or seashore? Bring along a welcome housegift collection of quilt, potholder, and recipe card. Add the basic ingredients and a coordinated rolling pin and pie plate. Then, spend a day picking blueberries for a well-deserved vacation treat.

Apple Harvest

Enjoy autumn's harvest with the pick of the crop—apples to quilt and cook.

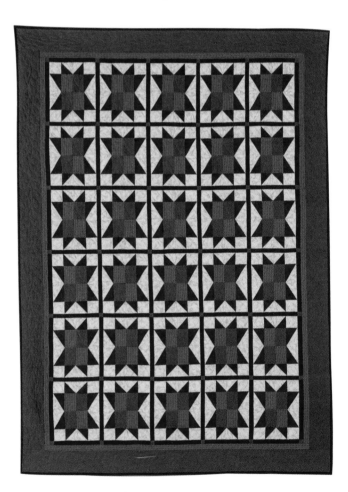

Apple Harvest Quilt

Apple Harvest Quilt

Finished Size: 54-1/2" x 75-1/2"
Finished Star Block: 8" x 10"

Supplies

2-5/8 yards Background

1-1/2 yards Green

7/8 yard Gold

3-1/2 yards Red

3-2/3 yard Backing

Cutting

Background
- 4—4-1/2" x 42" strips cut into 60—4-1/2" x 2-1/2" pieces
- 60—Template A
- 8—2-1/2" x 42" strips cut into 120—2-1/2" squares

Green
- 6—1-1/4" squares
- 2—1-1/4" x 42" strips
- 5—2-1/2" x 42" strips
- 2—4-1/2" x 67-3/4" strips for side borders
- 2—4-1/2" x 55" strips for top and bottom borders

Gold
- 5—2-1/2" x 42" strips
- 2—1-1/2" x 65-3/4" strips for side accent borders
- 2—1-1/2" x 47" strips for top and bottom accent borders

Red
- 8—2-1/2" x 42" strips cut into 120—2-1/2" squares (on the wrong side of the fabric, draw a line once on the diagonal)
- 60—Template B
- 60—Template B Reversed
- 1—8-1/2" x 42" strip cut into 35—1-1/2" x 8-1/2" pieces
- 2—10-1/2" x 42" strips
- 7—2-1/2" x 42" strips (binding)

Sewing

1. Using the 2-1/2" x 42" green and gold strips, make five strip sets. Cut into 60—3-1/2" Units A.

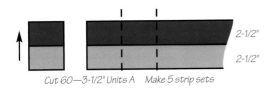

Cut 60—3-1/2" Units A   Make 5 strip sets

2. Sew Units A together, using opposing seams to make Block Center.

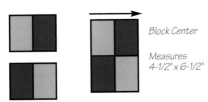

Block Center

Measures 4-1/2" x 6-1/2"

3. To make Small Star Points, sew 2-1/2" red squares, RST, to left side of 4-1/2" x 2-1/2" background pieces. Cut away 1/4" from drawn line. Press toward red. Repeat for right side. Make 60 Units B.

2-1/2"

4-1/2" x 2-1/2"

Make 60 Units B

4. To make Large Star Points, sew Template B, RST, to left side of Template A (refer to page 54). Press towards red. Sew Template B Reverse to right side. Press to red. Make 60 Units C.

Make 60 Units C

5. Sew 2-1/2" background squares to each end of Unit C.

2-1/2"

Assemble the Blocks

1. Sew Units B to the top and bottom of block center.

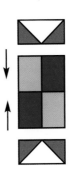

2. Sew Units C to each side of the block.

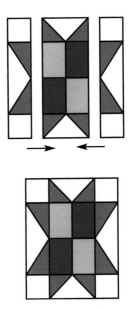

Assemble the Quilt

1. Sew 1-1/4" x 8-1/2" red sashing pieces to join five rows with six blocks in each. Press away from block.

2. Make two strip sets using 1-1/4" x 42" green and 10-1/2" x 42" red strips. Cut into 36—1-1/4" Units D.

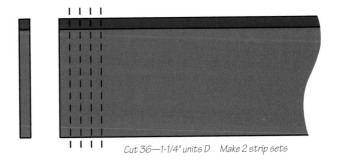

Cut 36—1-1/4" units D   Make 2 strip sets

3. Sew six Units D together and add 1-1/4" green square to end to make six sashing rows. Press to red.

4. Join rows with the sashing rows, add the 1-1/2"gold accent strips and 4-1/2" border strips, sides first then top and bottom. Press borders to outside.

4-1/2" x 67-3/4"

1-1/2" x 65-3/4"

1-1/2" x 47"

4-1/2" x 55"

Finishing the Quilt

See General Instructions on page 7 to layer, quilt, and bind.

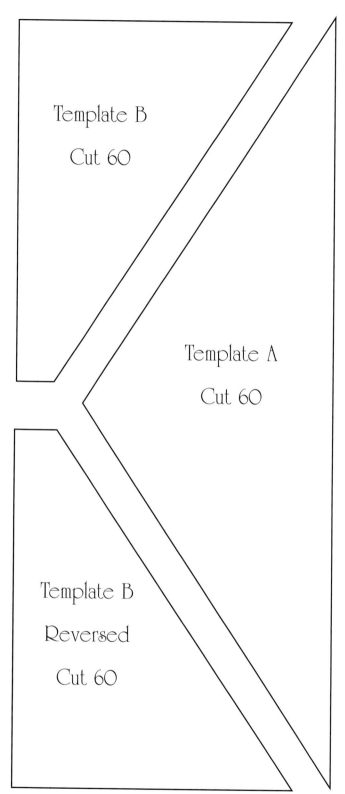

Template B

Cut 60

Template A

Cut 60

Template B

Reversed

Cut 60

Apple Harvest Quilt

Checkerboard Placemat

Finished Size: 16" x 12"

Supplies

Green: 1/4 yard

Orange: 1/4 yard

Red: 2/3 yard

Batting: 16-1/2" x 12-1/2" piece

Cutting

- Green: 3—2-1/2" x 22" strips
- Orange: 3—2-1/2" x 22" strips
- Red: 2—2-1/2" x 42" strips (binding) and
  1—16-1/2" x 12-1/2" piece (backing)

Sewing

1. Make one strip set using 2-1/2" x 22" green and orange strips. Cut into 8—2-1/2" Units A.

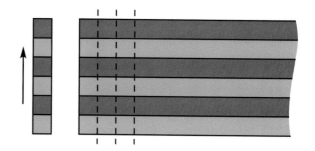

2. Sew units A together reversing direction of units.

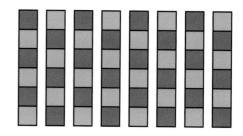

3. Lay placemat on batting piece and quilt. Trim edges even, and then bind same as quilt.

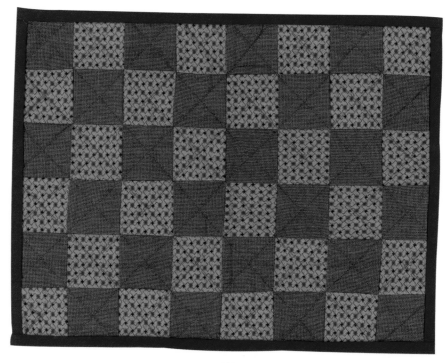

Checkerboard Potholder

Finished size: 9" oval

Supplies

Scraps of Red and Orange
Green - 1/2 yard
1 - 10" square of batting

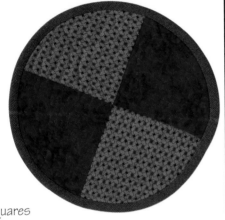

Cutting

- Red: 2— 5" squares
- Orange: 2—5" squares
- Green: 1—2-1/2" x 28" bias strip and
  1—10" square for backing

Sewing

1. Sew 5" squares together.

2. Cut pattern B, on
   fold, from squares
   and 10" square of
   backing and batting.

3. Layer top and backing
   (wrong sides together)
   with batting piece in
   between. Baste all layers 1/8" from
   edges around outside edge.

4. Quilt, then bind same as quilt.

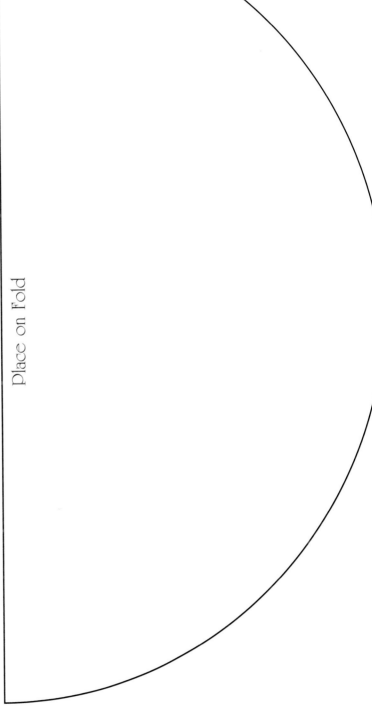

Place on Fold

Apple Harvest Pie

6 cups peeled sliced apples

3/4 cup white sugar

1 tsp. cinnamon

1/2 tsp. nutmeg

1–9" pie shell

In large mixing bowl, combine apples, sugar, and spices. Pour into unbaked pie shell.
Topping: Cream 1/2 cup brown sugar, and 1/2 cup butter. Using fork or pastry blender, cut in
1 cup flour. Sprinkle over apples. Bake in 375°oven 40 minutes, or until apples are tender.
Serves 8. Garnish with fried apple slices, if desired.

Recipe Card & Quilt Label

HOME COOKING

For a back-to-school treat,
try an apple for the teacher.
Fill a basket with crisp red
apples and add a greeting
for the teacher, a sure recipe for
getting the new school year
off to a great start.

Pumpkin Patch

These patchwork and embroidery treats will be the pick of the patch.

Pumpkin Patch Quilt

Pumpkin Patch Quilt

Finished Size: 50" x 74"
Finished Block: 12"

Supplies

3 yards Background

1 yard Gold color #1

1-7/8 yard Plaid color #2

1-5/8 yard Brown color #3

3-1/4 yards Backing

Cutting

Background
- 2—6-1/2" x 42" strips cut into 16—3-1/2" x 6-1/2" pieces
- 10—3-1/2" x 42" strips cut into 120—3-1/2" squares (on wrong side of the fabric, draw a line once on the diagonal)
- 16—1-1/2" x 42" strips
- 6—2-1/2" x 42" strips

Gold #1
- 3—6-1/2" x 42" strips cut into 28—3-1/2" x 6-1/2" pieces
- 2—1-1/2" x 66-1/2" sides
- 2—1-1/2" x 44-1/2" top and bottom

Plaid #2
- 3—6-1/2" x 42" strips cut into 32—3-1/2" x 6-1/2" pieces
- 10—1-1/2" x 42" strips
- 3—2-1/2" x 42" strips
- 6—2-1/2" x 42" strips (binding)

Brown #3
- 10—1-1/2"x 42" strips
- 3—2-1/2" x 42" strips
- 2—3-1/2" x 68-1/2" sides
- 2—3-1/2" x 50-1/2" top and bottom

Sewing

1. Make one each strip set using #2—2-1/2" x 42" strips and 2-1/2" x 42" background strips. Cut into 14—2 1/2" units and 7—2-1/2" units for Block 1.

Block 1
14—2-1/2" Units   *Make 1 strip set*

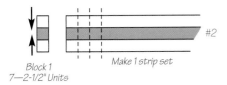

Block 1
7—2-1/2" Units   *Make 1 strip set*

A. Assemble 7 Large Nine - Patch Block 1.

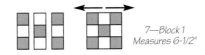

7—Block 1
Measures 6-1/2"

2. Make one each strip set using #3—2-1/2" x 42" strips and 2-1/2" x 42" background strips. Cut into 16—2-1/2" units and 8—2-1/2" units for Block 2.

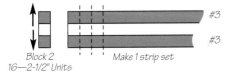

Block 2
16—2-1/2" Units   *Make 1 strip set*

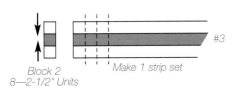

Block 2
8—2-1/2" Units   *Make 1 strip set*

A. Assemble 8 Large Nine - Patch Block 2.

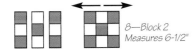

8—Block 2
Measures 6-1/2"

3. Make four strip sets using #2—1-1/2" x 42" strips and 1-1/2" x 42" background strips. Cut into 96—1-1/2" units.

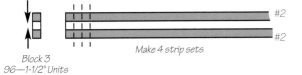

Block 3
96—1-1/2" Units   *Make 4 strip sets*

A. Make two strip sets using #2—1-1/2" x 42" strips and 1-1/2" x 42" background strips. Cut into 48—1-1/2" units.

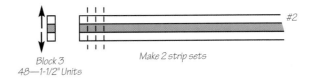

Block 3
48—1-1/2" Units   *Make 2 strip sets*

B. Assemble 48 Small Nine - Patch Block 3.

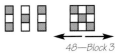

48—Block 3

4. Make four strip sets using #3—1-1/2" x 42" strips and 1-1/2" x 42" background strips. Cut into 96—1-1/2" units.

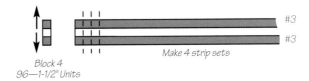

Block 4
96—1-1/2" Units   *Make 4 strip sets*

A. Make two strip sets using #3—1-1/2" x 42" strips and 1-1/2" x 42" background strips. Cut into 48—1-1/2" units.

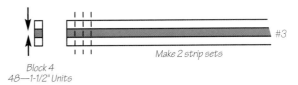

Block 4
48—1-1/2" Units   *Make 2 strip sets*

B. Assemble 48 Small Nine - Patch Block 4.

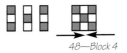

48—Block 4

5. Using Small Nine - Patch Block 3 and 3-1/2" x 6-1/2" background pieces make 10 sashing strips.

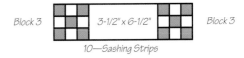

Block 3   3-1/2" x 6-1/2"   Block 3
10—Sashing Strips

A. Using Small Nine - Patch Block 4 and 3-1/2" x 6-1/2" background pieces make 6 sashing strips.

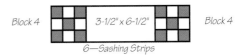

Block 4   3-1/2" x 6-1/2"   Block 4
6—Sashing Strips

B. Assemble top and bottom sashing strips.

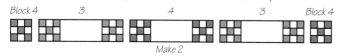

Make 2

6. Place 3-1/2" background squares, RST, on left side of #1 3-1/2" x 6-1/2" piece. Sew on drawn line. Cut away 1/4" from sewn line. Press out. Repeat for right side. Make 28 units.

A. Repeat for color #2. Make 32 units.

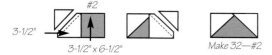

7. To each end of color #1 unit, sew Small Nine - Patch Block 3. Make 14.

A. Repeat for color #2 unit adding Small Nine Patch Block #4. Make 16.

8. To each side of Large Nine - Patch Block #1 add color #1 units. Make 7.

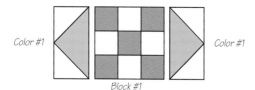

A. Repeat for Large Nine - Patch Block #2 adding color #2 units. Make 8.

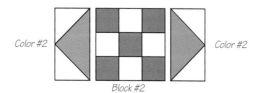

9. Assemble Large Block #1 using colors #1 and #2. Make 7.

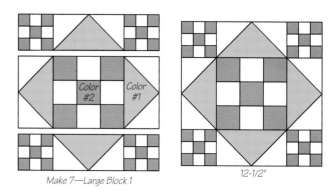

Make 7—Large Block 1   *12-1/2"*

A. Assemble Large Block #2 using colors #2 and #3. Make 8.

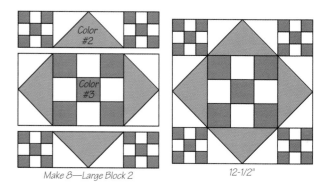

Make 8—Large Block 2   *12-1/2"*

Assemble the Quilt

1. Sew #2 Small Nine - Patch sashing strips and #3 Small Nine - Patch sashing strips using illustration below.

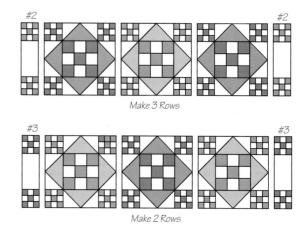

Make 3 Rows

Make 2 Rows

2. Assemble rows, then add top and bottom Small Nine - Patch sashing strips.

A. Add 1-1/2" accent borders then 3-1/2" outside borders, sides first then top and bottom.

Finishing the Quilt

See General Instructions on page 7 to layer, quilt, and bind.

Pumpkin Patch Quilt

Pumpkin Patch Table Runner

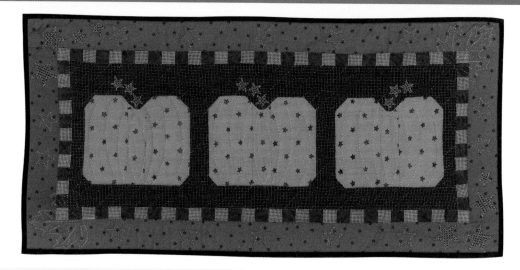

Finished Size: 38" x 18"

Supplies

Background—1/3 yard

Stars—1/4 yard

Checkerboard—1/8 yard each, light and dark

Border—1/4 yard

Backing—5/8 yard

Binding—1/4 yard

Fusible Web—1/4 yard (optional)

6 medium size buttons if desired

Cutting

- Background: 6—1" squares,
  6—1-1/4" squares,
  6—1-1/2" squares,
  3—2" x 1-1/2" pieces,
  2—1-3/4" x 7-1/4" pieces,
  2—2" x 7-1/4" pieces,
  1—31-1/2" x 1-3/4" strip, and
  1—31-1/2" x 3-1/2" strip

- Pumpkins: 6—1" squares,
  6—4" x 7-1/4" pieces, and
  3—2" x 6-1/4" pieces

- Checkerboard: 2—1-1/2" x 42" strips each, light and dark

- Border: 2—3" x 18-1/2" strips and
  2—3" x 33-1/2" strips

- Binding: 3—2-1/2" x 42" strips

Sewing

1. RST, sew 1-1/2", 1-1/4", and 1" background squares to the 4" x 7-1/4" pumpkin pieces as shown. Make three each left and right sides.

1-1/2" 1" 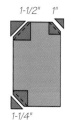  1 1"-1/2"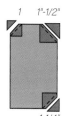

1-1/4" Left Side Make 3 1-1/4" Right Side Make 3

2. Sew two 1" pumpkin squares to one 2" x 1-1/2" background pieces. Make three. Sew these to 2" x 6-1/4" pumpkin pieces.

2" x 1-1/2"

 2" x 6-1/4"

Make 3

3. Assemble the pumpkin pieces. Make three pumpkins. Each will measure 9" x 7-1/4".

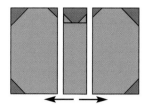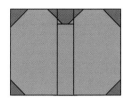

4. Sew the 1-1/2" x 42" light and dark strips together to make one strip set. Cut into 22—1-1/2" units.

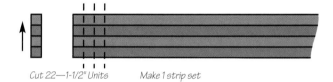

Cut 22—1-1/2" Units   Make 1 strip set

A. Sew units end to end and make two rows of 11 count units and two rows of 33 count units. Press all one direction.

Make 2—11 Count

Make 2—33 Count

5. Join the pumpkins and top and bottom strips as shown in the illustration.

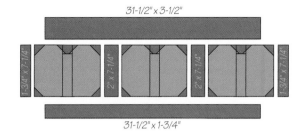

31-1/2" x 3-1/2"

31-1/2" x 1-3/4"

6. Add the 11-count checkerboard to the sides and the 33-count to the top and bottom. Sew on 3" top and bottom, then side borders.

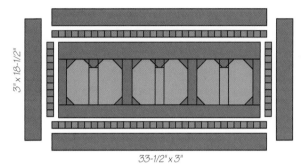

3" x 18-1/2"

33-1/2" x 3"

7. Hand appliqué or fuse stars in place. **Optional: place a button in the center of large stars. Layer quilt and bind.

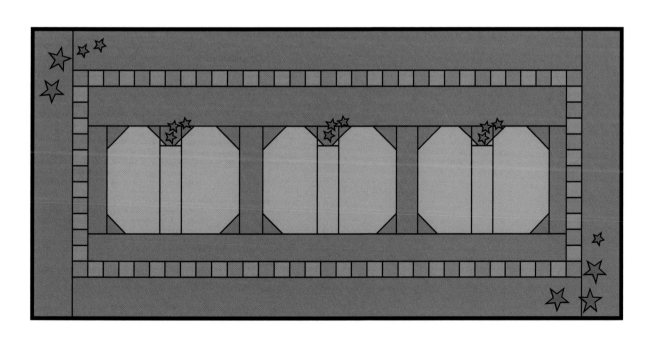

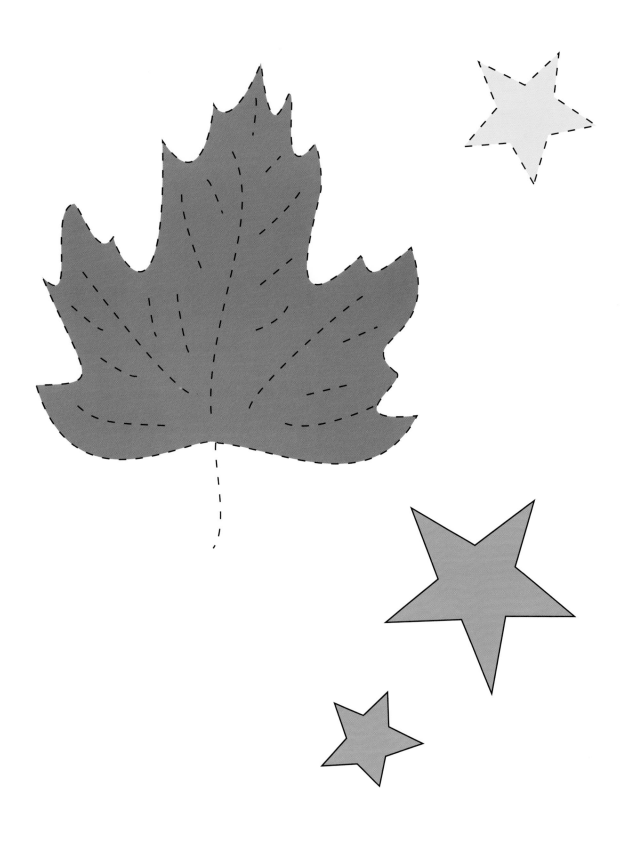

Pumpkin Patch Appliqué and Quilting Patterns

Placemat

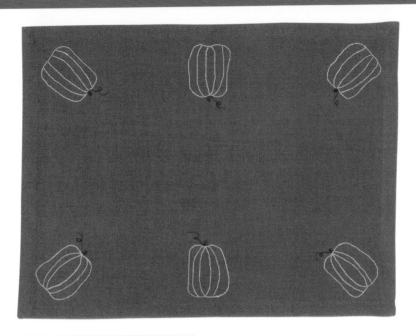

Supplies

Purchased Placemat

1 - skein cream or orange floss for pumpkin

1 - skein green floss for stem and tendril

Sewing

1. Transfer pattern evenly around placemat. To transfer pattern cut out pumpkin shape and trace outside shape onto placemat. Free hand draw pumpkin sections to inside of shape.

2. Using two strands of floss, satin stitch the stem and back stitch the tendrils and pumpkins.

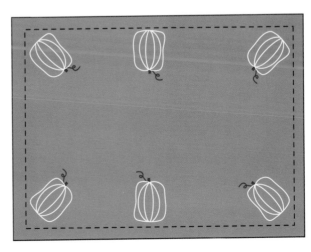

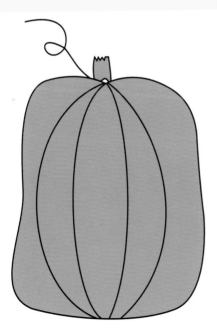

Pumpkin Patch Pie

1-1/2 cups canned pumpkin

3/4 cup dark brown sugar

1/2 tsp. salt

1/2 tsp. ginger

1 tsp. cinnamon

3 slightly beaten eggs

2 cups light cream

1—9" pie shell

whipped cream (optional)

ice cream (optional)

In large mixing bowl combine pumpkin, sugar, salt, and spices. Add eggs and cream. Pour into prepared 9" pie shell. Bake in 450°oven 10 minutes, then in 325°oven about 30 minutes, or until knife comes out clean. Serve warm or cold with ice cream or sweetened whipped cream. Serves 8.

Recipe Card & Quilt Label

Display the pumpkin patch quilt on the dining room wall and dress up your harvest table with a coordinating table runner, place-mat and perfect pumpkin pie. Use the recipe card as a place card by writing the guest's name on the front and including the recipe on the inside of the fold-over card.

Strawberry Surprise

Surprise your holiday guests with *edible snowflakes* in a coconut-filled pie.

Strawberry Surprise Quilt

Strawberry Surprise Quilt

Finished Size: 50-1/4" x 63"
Finished Piece and Alternating Block: 9" x 9"

Supplies

2-1/2 yards Background

10 Fat Quarters:
2 - Dark Red;
2 - Medium Red; 1 - Light Red
2 - Dark Pink; 2 - Medium Pink
1 - Light Pink

1 yard Accent Border and Binding

1-1/3 yards Backing

Cutting

Background
- 1—5-1/2" x 42" strip cut into
  6—5-1/2" x 9-1/2" pieces
- 2—5-1/2" x 22" strips
- 2—8" x 22" strips
- 2—7-1/2" squares cut once on the diagonal
  for corner triangles
- 3—13" squares cut twice on the diagonal
  for setting triangles
- 2—4-1/2" x 55-1/2" strips for side borders
- 2—4-1/2" x 50-3/4" strips for top and
  bottom borders

Fat Quarters: From each of the fat quarters:
- 3—1-1/2" x 22" strips

From three different reds
- 3 each—5-1/2" x 22" strips
- 3 each—2-1/2" x 22" strips cut into
  8 each—5-1/2" x 2-1/2" pieces

From three pinks
- 2 each—2-1/2" x 22" strips

From same medium red
- 6—2-1/2" x 22" strips

Accent and Binding
- 2—2-1/2" x 51-1/2" strips for side borders
- 2—2-1/2" x 42-3/4" strips for top
  and bottom borders
- 6—2-1/2" x 42" strips for binding

Sewing

Blocks I

1. Make 5 strip sets, 5 strips in each, randomly placing the 1-1/2" x 22" strips. Cut into 60—1-1/2" units.

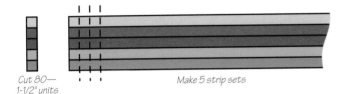

Cut 80—1-1/2" units *Make 5 strip sets*

A. Sew 5—1-1/2" units together, alternating pressing direction, to make 12—Center Blocks I. Press one direction.

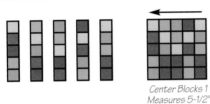

Center Blocks 1
Measures 5-1/2"

2. Make 3 strip sets using same 2-1/2" x 22" pink strips and same 5 1/2" x 22" red strips. Cut into 8—2-1/2" units, from each strip set. Total 24 units.

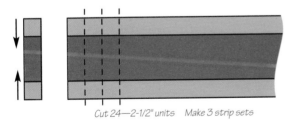

Cut 24—2-1/2" units   *Make 3 strip sets*

A. Sew same 5-1/2" x 2-1/2" red pieces to top and bottom of Center Blocks I, then add same 2-1/2" units to complete three each color Blocks I. Total 12 blocks.

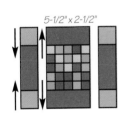

5-1/2" x 2-1/2"

12—Center Blocks 1
Measures 9-1/2"

Blocks II

1. Make 2 strip sets, using same 2-1/2" x 22" medium red and 5-1/2" x 22" background strips. Cut into 12—2-1/2" units.

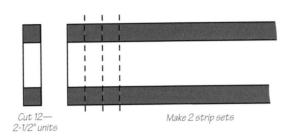

Cut 12—2-1/2" units   *Make 2 strip sets*

A. Sew units to 5-1/2" x 9-1/2" background pieces to complete 6 Blocks II.

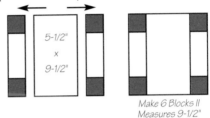

5-1/2"
x
9-1/2"

Make 6 Blocks II
Measures 9-1/2"

Setting Triangles

1. Make two strip sets using 2-1/2" x 22" medium red, used in Blocks II, and 8" background strips. Cut into 10—2-1/2" units.

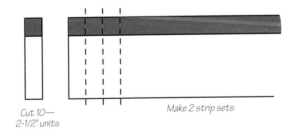

Cut 10—2-1/2" units   *Make 2 strip sets*

A. Add 2-1/2" units to setting triangles. Make 6—Setting Triangles A.

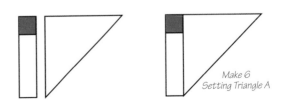

Make 6
Setting Triangle A

B. Add 2-1/2" units to setting triangles.
Make 4—Setting Triangles B.

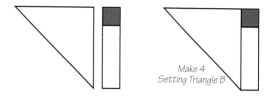

Make 4
Setting Triangle B

Assemble the Quilt

1. Using illustration as a guide, sew Blocks I and II together and add setting triangles to blocks. Add corner triangles last. Trim edges of quilt 1/4" from outside pink points. Stitch 1/8" around outside edges of quilt to prevent stretching.

2. Add 2 1/2" accent borders, then 4-1/2" outside borders, sides first then top and bottom borders.

4-1/2" x 55-1/2"

4-1/2" x 50-3/4"

Finishing the Quilt

See General Instructions on page 7 to layer, quilt, and bind.

Strawberry Surprise Quilt

Strawberry Sachets

3. Center leaf on top and with long needle and long piece of floss, tack leaves with one stitch. Come up through center top and tie off several times, cutting threads 1-1/2" long.

Supplies

Scraps (extra blocks cut up)

Handful of stuffing

Green floss

Cutting

- 4—strawberry pattern pieces (all the same or alternating colors 2 - each)
- 1—Leaf pattern piece

Sewing

1. Sew two strawberry pattern pieces together on straight side. Press one direction. Repeat and press opposite direction.

   A. Sew two pieces together, locking seams at bottom, leaving top open.

2. Turn right side out and gather top with quilting thread or string. Begin stuffing, pulling gather tighter as you get to the top. Gather tightly and tie off.

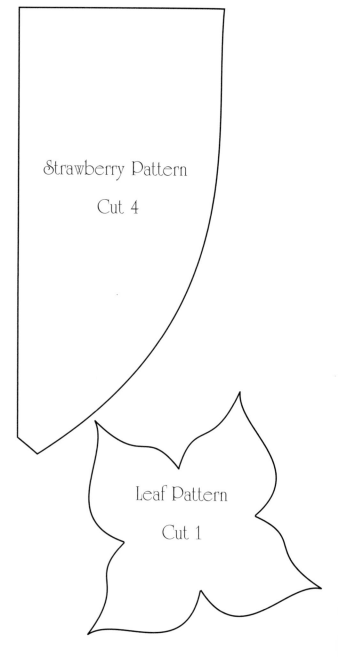

Strawberry Pattern

Cut 4

Leaf Pattern

Cut 1

Strawberry Surprise Pie

1/2 cup sugar

1/4 flour

1 envelope unflavored gelatin (1 T)

1/2 tsp. salt

1-3/4 cups milk

3/4 tsp. vanilla

1/4 tsp. almond flavoring

1/2 cup whipping cream, whipped

1 cup moist shredded coconut

Blend sugar, flour, gelatin and salt thoroughly in saucepan. Gradually stir in milk.

Cook over medium heat until mixture boils, stirring constantly. Boil 1 minute. Place in cold water. Cool until mixture mounds slightly when dropped from spoon.

Stir in vanilla and almond flavoring.

Fold in whipped cream, then coconut, being careful to use as few strokes as possible.

Carefully place mixture in prepared, cooled meringue shell. Sprinkle with moist shredded coconut. Chill several hours until set. Serve cold. Garnish with crushed strawberries or raspberries.

Meringue shell:
Preheat oven to 275°. Beat 3 egg whites and 1/4 tsp. cream of tartar until frothy.

Gradually add 1/2 cup sugar. Continue beating until sugar is dissolved and the mixture forms stiff peaks when beaters are removed. Do not under beat. Swirl mixture into a 9" pie pan, using back of a wooden spoon to shape the bowl.

Cook for 45 minutes. Cool completely before filling with above mixture.

Recipe Card & Quilt Label

Make this gift collection extra-special with a trio of strawberry sachets. Fill them with your favorite holiday potpourri and use the fold-over recipe card as a gift enclosure.